Call Me A Witch

Call Me A Witch

Riley Killen & Vaani Tiwari

Note: This is a work of fiction. Names, characters, places, and incidents are either the product of the author's imagination or used fictitiously, and any resemblance to actual persons, living or dead, business establishments, events, or locales is entirely coincidental.

Call Me A Witch copyright © 2026 by Vaani Tiwari and Riley Killen. All rights reserved. No part of this publication may be reproduced, distributed, or transmitted in any form or by any means, including photocopying, recording, or other electronic or mechanical methods, without the prior written permission of the authors, except in the case of brief quotations embodied in critical reviews and certain other noncommercial uses permitted by copyright law. Thank you for respecting these rights.

ISBN: 9798218904906 (Paperback)

Illustrations by Boya Liu
Cover art by Noor Latif
Designs by Vaani Tiwari & Riley Killen

For those who survived their own becoming.

Content Warnings: Contains themes of self harm, violence/gruesome imagery, suicidal ideation, mentions of guns, and brief nudity.

Prologue

There's a story of a ▮
▮ witch ▮
banished from the ▮
▮ land ▮.

▮ born ▮
and burned ▮
▮
▮

▮ wreathed in
▮ sin,
▮ most
certainly damned ▮
▮
▮ a predator ▮
▮.

▮ her blood-stained
lips ▮ were ▮
▮
a sign of evil; ▮
▮
▮ ruinous ▮

▮ the valiant villagers
rushed with swords raised
▮
▮
▮
certain ▮
▮
her death was required.

The men ▮ returned with
▮ torn stomachs,

███████████
███████████
██████
██████████████

████████████████████
█████████████ slaughtered
████ ██
and ██████████████████
██████████████ █████
██████ scorned;
██████████████████████
████████████████.

████████████████
this witch █████████████
has █ a cycle of blood ████
██████████████,
a wound ██████████
in shades of vermillion.

I. Fury

i am wrath

burn me, then.
burn what you cannot own,
what you could not break,
what you feared in the dark.
secretly, of course, because
how could a man be in the
wrong?

you needed a reason,
so you call me a witch,
because *woman* was not enough.

the flames cannot silence me
for ashes can't be unmade;
so i will wait.

i will be the smoke in your lungs,
settling behind your ribs,
crawling into your heart.

burn me, and
i will rise in every flame
you light to feel holy once more.

Anatomy of an Orchestra
after Skin & Bone by Vaani Tiwari

they melted me down
until i was nothing but
a pool of gold,
the petroleum in my mouth
running thicker than blood.
they gagged me—
yet demanded I sing.

fitted their mouths to the maw in my chest,
hollowed out my gilded bones and
blew tantara through ribcage,
a triumphant symphony
borne on red coals.
as i tarnished in the shape of
fingerprints and lips, they tilted my gaping mouth
to the heavens, a bellow like
tusked and battle-ready elephants,
rattling through me;
and as i bore their extravagance,
a vessel for their gaiety,
they exulted
"what a masterpiece."

as her petals fell

oh, what a daisy
pretty and lazy
that sunflower soul
just begging to be broke.

oh, what an animal
thoughtless, irrational
drink down your heart
and shatter the shot glass.

oh, what a machine
bitter and jade green
stay far away from
those vicious gray gears.

oh, what a monster
who would ever want her
with that ugly cracked smile
and lipstick-stained teeth.

oh, she's gone crazy
my, such a blaze she
creates as she detonates
in the silence of the wood—

you called her a witch,
nothing but a bitch;
well
just be glad
she chose to run
instead of picking up
your gun.

as i shattered (p2)

they said i fell.
no—
i was pushed,
tossed,
hurled
off the waterworn cliffs by
calloused hands i fought so hard
to bandage,
to wash,
to save.

you laughed as i tumbled,
my vision turning crimson,
swallowing bullets until i
hated myself so you wouldn't have to, until
they whispered *monster* and i clawed
at my reflection until i couldn't find her anymore.

is that what you wanted?

monster and
that word became
the only sound in the forest,
echoing off trees that bent away from me;

monster and
i stumbled
away, away from the mirrors you held
up to my face,
the ones where i saw your smile hiding
in my image;

monster and
i ripped the smoke-ruined voice from my
throat and threw it to the void,
but the void was only more full of you.

is
      this
            wh
                  at
                      y
                          o   u

                                              wanted?

lazy, they sneered, as i dragged my body through
their filth, their lies caked under my nails
scratching the words
      not
      enough
into my own skin. did they see
how heavy it was
to carry your words
like anchors in my throat? to hold my head
high as your stones crashed against it?

your favorite was to call me stone
but when I shattered, you couldn't bear my edges
cutting into you while you sifted through the debris,
searching for the girl you murdered
before this one. you cringed
away from the stench of burn-
ed flesh, of rage carved
into me by your dull knife
chewing until it spit out sparks
onto feverish skin.

you handed me your gun and
i stared down the barrel until
my reflection blinked first.

i wonder if you will ever
repent, or if you think
you are absolved just because
the trigger carries my fingerprints.

as the seasons turn (i)

springtime and she's
        sobbing because it all hurts,
        hurts so much more now that the
        sunshine has thawed the ice gathered on her
        moth-eaten bruises and torn away those threadbare
                        clouds from her fish-
                        belly pale skies.

with her back arched against blades of grass, she bleeds
        red (red roses they thought could gratify the grave)
        & as flowers break skin, she becomes—freckled with
        thorns—the hits landing black (black-eyed crows pecking
        at the breadcrumbs she laid) and blue (blue rivers eating through
        her raw-boned soil)

        & when she rises, bleeding beauty over their
        ugly, barren dirt, she will swallow

                              thunderclouds.

        & when she rains, she will do so with
           bared-   teeth   bitter-   ness.

the scream

bites away the staples holding down my curled edges
unstitching embroidered smile and open eyes
holding a quiet little match until my paper face blackens
sky-soaking me until i dissolve into a glass of ocean foam.

pours mortar into a footstep mold and drags me down to earth
with concrete slippers that aren't for dancing, but for marching
taking sticks and stones with child's fingers to make a scaffolding skeleton
pressing red brick walls into place, an empire downed and rebuilt
with the armor on the outside of a new land.

here in the new, it gathers in a square and cheers
plucking heartstrings one by one until they quiver
dragging a drumstick over the curved bones of my ribs.
tapping a quiet melody out over the keys of my collarbones
coaxing every inch of my skin to sing.

it unmakes me. it creates me. it obliterates
the prison bars stepping on my throat,
the iron brands around my wrists.
thrown in the sea and chained to stones,
one does not have the time or the breath
to become a lockpick when they have a
hammer instead.

standing throat bared, jaw open, teeth smashed and chest caving in,
arms out wide like anger or embrace or wings
swallowed by the sky and spitting out the blood until you're something
malleable newborn, steel-boned veteran, unmoving and fluid, this
is what the scream does.

Supernova

She found me fallen off the edge of the universe,
screaming into the void. We could never be
mistaken about each other, and

yet. She was an acoustic echo of myself,
mouth hung curiously at the torn-open,
star-stitched sight of me:
bleedingly beautiful and sucker-punched,
pearled teeth unsmiling, a fighter who learned and
unlearned how to

flinch. The void cracks with the force of me;
here I spin in my lonely infinities,
vicious in my helplessness. Whose anger
is this— worn on proud display
like a whale bone corset,
gnawing in on every

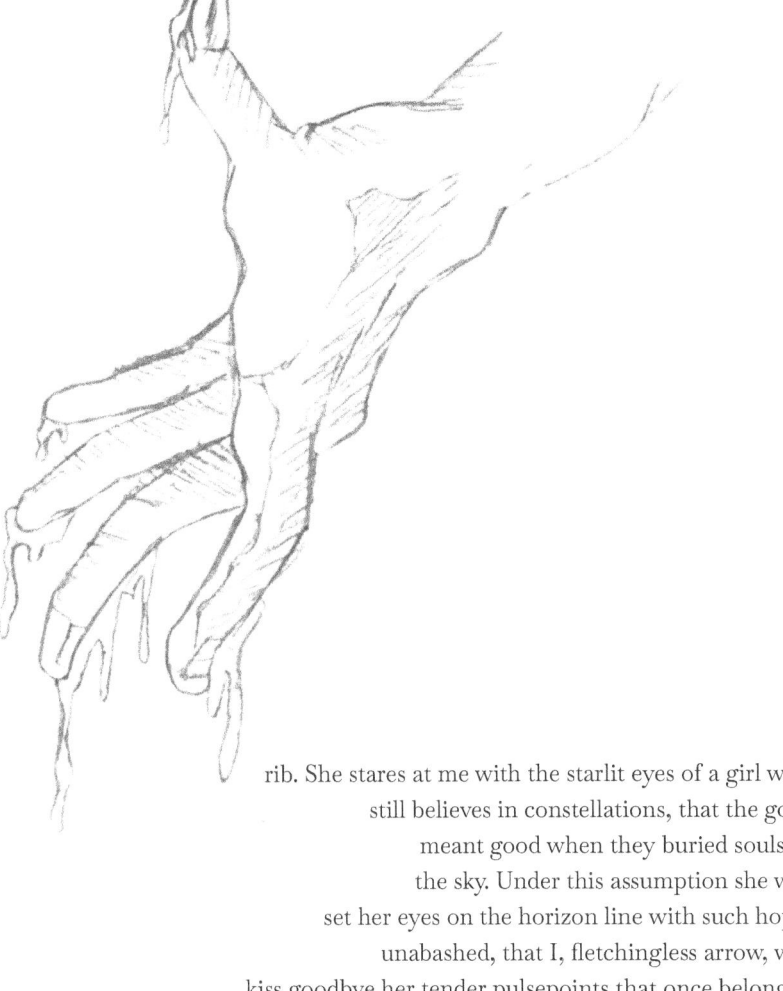

rib. She stares at me with the starlit eyes of a girl who
still believes in constellations, that the gods
meant good when they buried souls in
the sky. Under this assumption she will
set her eyes on the horizon line with such hope,
unabashed, that I, fletchingless arrow, will
kiss goodbye her tender pulsepoints that once belonged
to me—gone. When did I lose this? As if, even now,
I know enough to demand

these answers from her. The questions
break my teeth, so I
chew & chew until my smile is
hideous.

In a mirror, we could never be mistaken
for each other.

Iron & Fire

she balances on the precipice
fighting tooth and nail,
daring the dark to swallow her whole:

she's tasted its bite before
and come out spitting sparks.

they said she'd break, crumble;
a girl isn't made for the weight of
a world that enforces iron convictions.

but they never saw her claws,
sharpened into cruel blades,
ready to rip the night in two.

There will come a point, however, when her spite fails her. Her fury will still be thrashing somewhere—small, pathetic, and desperate, but hers.

She thinks.

Eventually, her hands will begin to scrabble at nothing, legs trembling under an intangible weight. One after another, her knees will buckle, darkness crushing her body and seeping into her skin. The shadows swirling around salivate in anticipation, ready to consume.

And eventually she will consider letting go; after all, despite her bravado, it was only a matter of time.

Quicksilver Girl

and so she fell;
back to the shadows from whence she
came screaming, so suddenly
dragged from snow-globe sanctity and
edenic innocence into a land lacking
forgiveness for sins she knew not existed—
grieving the simplicity and
honeyed embrace of ignorance. She
isn't one to break glass ceilings;
just bend them, on occasion. And yet, for her,
kindness has become an answerless query,
lost between scars and
mangled beyond recognition. This new world cares
not of who she was before, too misgiven of the
provocative thing they see her becoming. But do not be deceived;
quicksilver girls like her need no one's pity. And
rest assured, she receives none, for
she has already surrendered, become molten— if they
touch her, they'll blister, blame and cry. Should they look
under her skin, they'd find naught but
vermin hung from her bones,
weight dragging her down. These
x's over her eyes, she borrowed them from
yesterday's fallen and forgotten
zeroes, the ones before her,

        and now she wears them loudly.

II. Darkness

Flowers and Poison

i think i'm a monster.

i don't mean to be, but i am. i crave love the way fire craves air, devouring everything in my path to keep the flame alive. i see someone—a smile, a glance, a moment where they stumble—and suddenly i'm drawn to them. i pull them close, so close, until they're opening up for me like a flower, soft and trembling under my hands.

they think i'm the sun. they think i'm *theirs*.

and i let them.

i unravel their walls, peel back their layers, and hold the rawest, most fragile parts of them in my hands. they bloom for me, and i drink it in, and for a moment, it's enough. for a moment, i think, *this could be everything*.

but it's not. it never is. because there's always something else. someone else. something new and gleaming and thrilling that pulls me away.

so i let go.

i promise we'll catch up soon, we'll hang out soon, *i swear*. but the days stretch into weeks, and i drift further and further until they're left holding onto a love i've already walked away from.

they think i'm their person. their closest, their most intimate, but i already found my irreplaceables.

three people. three people i would hold onto with bloodied hands, even as the world burned itself to ash. my best friend, my constant, my north star. and the two others, my home, my safety, my *always*. they are the only ones who feel like forever. the only one i would never, *could never,* leave behind.

but they're so far away.

and when the hollow where they should be starts to ache too much, i try to fill it. i pull people in. i love them fiercely, intensely, desperately—but not enough. never enough. because the love i give them is different, quieter, fleeting. to them, it's everything. to me, it's... not.

and i hate myself for it.

because i know what it's like to be left behind. i know what it's like to wait for a text that never comes, to hold onto a connection that's already faded. and yet i do it to them. over and over, i do it to them.

i'm a monster because i still love them, even as i leave them behind. i love them, even as i move on to the next. i love them, even as they sit there with their hands outstretched and their hearts still open, waiting for something i can't give.

and no matter how much i love, it's never enough. i am never enough.

so, tell me: does that make me cruel? does that make me selfish? does that make me something worse?

& if it does, then maybe i deserve to be left behind too.

unwanted

you'll find her under the table
breaking her teeth on the stale scraps of your love
                        (when you remember to throw
                        them)
but dropping everything to spare you a bloody smile.
she is the colour of a plum;
cut open, yellow, raw, bruised
                        (used).
sometimes you find it in yourself to duck under the
table cloth and draw a laugh out of her mouth
but when you resurface, it with her grime caked under your nails
and you leave her in her self-imposed exile
                        (forget her so easily;
                        out of sight out of mind,
                        and you're so much lighter that way,
                        without her on her knees at your feet).

the thing is:
    you think that if she didn't belong so completely to you
    you might be able to appreciate her smile when it comes
    but as it is her smile with never just be teeth to you;
    it's a noose, holding you above her like some sort of gruesome
    tether to heaven. but even then in your matching bruises you
    hold yourself apart, touching the ring choking your throat
    and avoiding the sight of her split knees,
    even though you'd rather look at those then her eyes because if
    she's human to you it makes it harder to turn your back,
    because you know she'll cry in secret. when she's not performing
    like a circus lion you chance a look and see nothing but a
    starving dog, desperate for love and certain that if she just
    unstitches herself into something a little grander, a little
    better, then she'll be able to fit herself into the grand illusion
    she's painted around you
                    so artistic, but the saddest thing is that
                    you might like her more if she stopped
              trying to unmake herself
              for you.
maybe the worst part is even after seeing her guts as she
unspools herself and tries again and again in vivid and gruesome
detail, even when she's unbearably and utterly human to you,
you still
don't
    w
       a
          n
            t
her?

gold and pyrite

                                          love & hate look the same when
                                                        you're underwater

they were shackle and wrist

                                                they both hold you under

from the moment they first kissed

                                                      until you become

shackles bound, wrists rubbed raw

                                               a flowerbed for bruises

sinking like stones at the whim of the law

                                             you will press fingers to

the shackle begs *stay*

                                      following the shapes & pretending

the wrist sobs *let go*

                                          they're proof you're still wanted

bubbles streaming from both mouths

                                          even when you know better

as they fall further and further below

                  (at least parallel lines never had the chance to cut one another)

My mother's garden shears

well-oiled, ugly, starkly silver in an industrial way with bug-eyed screws through joints & rust-red handles. unapologetically selfish, an edge that looks you in the face as it cuts off your arm. just & merciful.

i am not my mother.

incandescent

when you find her you cannot help but stop
and stare
and feel helplessly like your hands are
empty.
and when you ask her for her name,
she turns her face up to the sun in such an
open-petaled smile as she says, *i am incandescent.*
You tell her that's not one of the options;
roll your eyes. But there she stands, thornless,
disgustingly content, and when you try to leave, you find that
she does not want to follow
(and you desperately want her to)
and so you
take her
        from her soil and
cut away her
        unseemly roots and
place her
        in the neck of a vase then
press her
        in between the pages of a book and
frame her
        between two slices of glass then
hang her
        on your wall,
        above your bed like a featherless
        dreamcatcher. you wait for her to thank you, but she no longer
laughs,
        and you should be able to sleep peacefully,
        right,
        without the unbearable sound
        grinding itself into your blood, but you can't stop yourself from
asking again

and again, *what are you,*
>*what*
>*are you,*
>the words bleeding straight
>from split lips onto her shut
>eyes, and you don't understand why it hurts when
>she no longer calls herself *incandescent,*
>even after you've made her
>into such a thing of light, sunlight trapped
>and refracting rainbows from
>where she hangs
>>encased in glass.

applause

i mistook their eyes for hands—
    thought if enough of them looked,
      i might feel held.

so i danced until the room
    forgot i had bones,
until i
forgot that i shared
more blood with ankles
devoured by stone than
      sky.

and by the time the clapping stopped,
    its violence could no longer be disguised by
    smiling faces. the sound fell and crack-
ed open on
novocain ears.
    i stayed bowed,
      trying to remember
      which face of mine
      they truly
believed.

the hunger

it grows teeth in the dark,
    gnarled and gleaming,
    tearing into the soft flesh of moments
    i thought were mine to savour.
    its mouth drips with everything
    i almost became.

it howls in technicolor:
    red flashes like a wound left open,
    blue seeps under my nails,
    purple bruises the air around my lungs.
    its voice scrapes the ceiling,
    a long, low scream
    that refuses to end.

i tried to bargain—
    fed it gold-leaf promises
    and the glittering bones of ambition,
    watched it swallow whole
    the sweetness of a quiet life.
    still, it claws at me,
    spits out the sun,
    says, *more.*

now it curls in my shadow,
    pressing sharp shoulders
    against the curve of my spine,
    and when i stand,

it stands with me,
    grinning,
        its belly still empty.

The Hollow Ache of Absence

sometimes it's like you died,
like you packed up your laughter,
your warmth, and
left
a hollow echo where you once stood.
i hate you for it,
for the way you left my life so quietly
like a shadow slipping
past dawn,
leaving me here with questions:
is my skin the wrong shade of love?

i'm left wondering if this ache is part of me,
if loneliness is stitched into my bones,
because the ones i love leave,
while i stay here, watching doors close, hating myself
for every goodbye.

and i want to ask you, beg you, if you're somewhere, listening—
am i unlovable?
is there something sharp in my soul, a blade i cannot see
which keeps you away,
or was i just the passing comfort, a hand to hold
until someone warmer came along?

and the silence mocks me, the empty spaces
you used to fill, like maybe it's my fault,
maybe this ache is all i deserve,
maybe i am the hollow, and the hollow
is me.

Skin Deep

i ruin myself because beauty feels like a lie, and i'd rather scar than be seen for what i am.

some girls are born with silk for skin, but mine came stitched in warnings. a fabric too loud for softness, too restless for rest. it itched. it blistered. it begged to be unmade, and so i answered. it was so simple; a thread pulled here, a seam split there until ruby rose through. what began as blemish ends as bloom. scabs rise like monuments, like proof of touch, of trespass, of trying.

no one saw the altar in it. the precision. the patience. how i turned my body into devotion and named bleeding as the offering.

some nights the mirror softens, and i catch a version of myself not yet ruined. almost lovely. almost— but my reflection lies in languages i never learned to trust, and beauty, when it settles, isn't something a girl like me deserves. so i flinch. i cleanse. i correct. and each time, my fingers come back crimson.

i've never prayed with hands that didn't tremble. never kissed a wound without tasting shame, but god, i have worshipped in silence— picking hymns from skin, singing please, let this be the last time i need to be forgiven.

still, the body remembers what it's been taught: that pain means penance, that stillness is surrender, that even lilies rot if you hold them too long. and i have held myself too long. too tight. too cruel. hoping one day i'll disappear just enough to be worth keeping.

Paper Cuts

They think words heal,
but mine bleed.
Every line I write
tears open a scar I thought had closed.
These pages are not a refuge;
they are a battlefield,
and my pen is a sword
too heavy for my hands.

Seams

I smile, but I am covered in seams. Look closer. Do you see? The fish-belly shine of my scalp, the crescent moons on my wrists. But it is in my heart where I wish the most there was a seam— for if I can't reach it, how can I make it clean?

Here is what I do: I press two clasped fists to the hard bone there and gasp, and gasp, and gasp; the clawed hands of my ribcage softly set their hands on the desk in front of them and study the thing trapped between them with a gentle, curious apathy, noting the way it thrashes; and gasp, and gasp, and gasp and— they will keep it there, pinned like a butterfly on a board: useful, beautiful, dead— and *gasp*.

The heart does not wish to die. It bucks its hips and tries its hardest to shatter every bone in my body. I, the frame, do not matter to it as it beats its chitin wings, blowing to fairy dust with every gust in its raw hope that it might someday crack the glass that encases it. I, the glass, am nothing but the resentful shackles keeping it from rapture. I, the vessel, will be bruised into a black-blue night sky on my tender inside from its savagery.

Someday it will beat without the bars of my ribs, the flesh muffling its screams, the body tying it down. It wouldn't beat long, but somehow, I think it would find the bargain worthwhile. Those moments of freedom would be the best it ever got to have. After all— while it pumps oxygen, I am the one who tastes the piercing cold of a winter-sky breath, drawn deep into aching lungs. While it is filled with blood, it will never feel the salt of a wound tearing open lush flesh. It will never taste the kiss it compelled me to steal, nor fall to its knees when that kiss leaves with my love, my cheeks wet and my mouth empty.

My mouth is another seam. That is where I drink, and dream. They taught those girls to keep theirs shut, afraid of what might escape; my open mouth found my heart's vestiges long ago, and this is where we meet in the middle, groping about blindly for each other's pinkie fingers with that old, salvaged earnestness.

(That is where everything is taken, and given. Somewhere along the way, we lost track and now we don't know which is which).

metamorphosis

w
h
a
t
if
this
thing break-
ing (around) me is the
chrysalis & not
the cocoon? or
could it be both heart-
break & freedom
as my wings punch through
these paper walls, leaving soft knuckles
bloody, daft heart scabbed & flinching, wondering
if this is a terrible m i s t a k e oh god what have i done,
i miss caterpillar flightlessness, letting my mind kiss the thought
of the sky until it was reinvented, i'd take the sole of a kinder boot than the
soul
i have sent scattering the blue and grieving the green
is this supposed to be growth? am i supposed to be thankful?
that i'm soaring & solitary? i'm adrift in the winds. i was always lost to myself
but now my eyes collide again & again inevitably with my own emptiness
no more cheap green leaves to stuff my ravenous mouth
and so here i am. the destroyer of the life i wrapped
so lovingly around myself.
the discarder of the things
i loved most. maybe i was
lost. maybe i was
small. but now
they're gone.
and it's not
worth
t
h
i
s

III. Burnout

kindness

i am such a
punching bag beggar when it comes down to
the fight mat on the floor, my blood on the dirt
my teeth in your knuckles, my smile ground to sand
under your Achilles heel, the sound of me drowned,
two hands laced together just to be crushed by your boot.

i'm trying, ok, i swear i am, but how can i end this war
without becoming it? has there ever been a war fought for
good? can burned things be saved? or just forgotten?

but you've had far too many take an eye for an eye,
leaving you blinded in pain and lost in darkness,
the unknown making you scared enough to gnaw off
both your helper's hands before you reckon yourself free.

it's alright.
i have a hand to spare, if you like.
it's worth it because my eyes are open and i see you
for the lost treasure, shipwrecked, sunken thing that you are.
not a monster. but simply something achingly human
begging for a shield from the world for a moment
before you're overcome by it.

i'll be the horse's mane, the lizard's tail,
the thing to take the teeth and the claws
that will fall away when you get your legs under you.
i'll watch you walk and
swim and
run.

don't forget me,
because i'm the best thing down here, maybe even the best thing
ever, and that's *why* i'm down here, if there's no rest for the
wicked, maybe i'm the wickedest thing out there.

i think it'd be true if i were looking in a mirror.

it always takes me a moment to get back up.
no matter what lovely handholds they make,
the knives wedged in my spine still bleed,
red fading into the soft mud that encases me
in a gentle cold that says, it's okay, it's alright,
and tries to wrap its arms around me tenderly
enough that i can still breathe.

but i will.
because there will always be someone else who needs me. always
another fist aching for a hand to hold, knuckles that must be bruised
before they are kissed, and after all this time, i find
it's better if i convince myself that i don't mind
being the thing they burn so that they can be reborn.

but something. that i did used to wonder. before this all become routine–
maybe the first couple or thousand or millions of times–
if someday it finally breaks me and i can't find it in myself to swim
without hope of ever reaching shore,
who will pick up my pieces when i'm one of the broken ones
down here?
who will be kind
to kindness?

Sting

i cried so hard last night
my eyes sting every time i blink—
like a punishment for feeling,
like salt pressed into a wound i didn't ask for.

there's an empty mug by my bed,
the tea's long gone cold.
its lip is cracked, jagged,
sharp enough to cut,
but i keep drinking anyway,
as if bitterness can fill the spaces
inside me that nothing else could.

the walls of this room know me better
than any friend i've ever had—
they've memorized the curve of my shadow,
the silence of my tongue,
the way my hands shake
when the clock hits 3 a.m.

and i'm tired, god, i'm so tired—
of the sting, the salt, the quiet,
the endless ache that wraps itself
around my bones like it owns me.

but i stay.
maybe out of spite,
maybe for the way the light
spills through the blinds
on a rare soft morning.
or maybe because i forgot how to leave—
and leaving feels harder
than the staying ever does.

The Weight of Wings

I tried to fly,
but my wings were heavy
with broken dreams.
Every feather carried a memory,
every bone a regret.
I wonder if I was ever meant to soar,
or if the sky was just another lie
I told myself to keep going.

Ash, Eventually

it lives in the quiet;
a flame barely breathing,
its amber skin trembling against the weight of the night.
i sit before it,
its light etching shadows into the hollows of my face,
its warmth pulling secrets from my ribs,
one by one, like petals plucked from a dying flower.

the fire is alive,
its flicker both fragile and eternal,
a fleeting moment stretched across lifetimes.
it dances as if it knows the ache of being seen—
how the world devours beauty,
how it watches and waits,
always ready to name a flicker a failure.

but the fire burns anyway.
not for the watching eyes,
not for the hands that built it.
it burns because it must.
because what else is there
but to consume,
to transform?

its flames whisper truths the world is too loud to hear:
that to flicker is not to falter,
that even the briefest light
can unravel the darkest sky.
it reminds me that we, too, are flames,
born to burn and be burned,
to give ourselves away in pieces
and call it living.

and yet, i fear the fire.
its hunger mirrors my own,
its longing to consume reflects
the hollows i carry like souvenirs.
what if i, too, am meant to turn to ash?
what if all i build
ends in smoke?

Yes.

should i be planting myself before the gaunt face of my clock
eyes narrowed into numbers counting down to judgement day
cracking my teeth on highlighters and bleeding myself gray,
give the color to a paper that will lose itself and forget faster than
my mouth can wrap the syllables *finished*.

should i screw myself into a lid and claw at the glass
until my wings shrivel up and i fall into dreams of
sand and sand and sand and sand and sand and then

should i stride out, wrists bare, with the red pen already uncapped
if it means i will never write something on the page?

or should i go out there
to the endless becoming:
worthlessness that makes me
smile for some strange reason,
things that lay naked of thought
or prayer, no knives or pens with which to carve
out a legacy— so stupid they are
lovely, they are blameless,
they are watching
me round-eyed as i
let my time waste
away until i'm under
water, cease my
incessant churning,
let the bubbles clear
needle my lenses, cut into
window frames through which to see the world;
let this current wipe me on the parted lips of the beach
as if i'm real.

or should i condemn myself
to nothing
in the necessity for both?

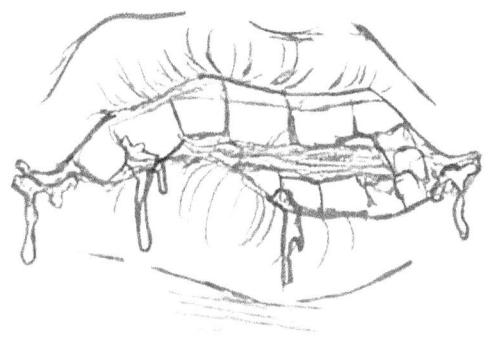

Tired

coverlets curled around my neck like a docile snake
coils shifting slowly enough that it feels like a hug
dipping me into the midnight tides of sleep until
i try to come up for air and find none.
this warm, sweet creature, basked in shadows
craving company and willing to kill to claim it
this soft, innocent thing, drowned in darkness
cramming its pleas for me to stay into my mouth
until my head is full of feathers and i'm falling like a bird
shot from the sky.
it's a toxic kind of love, a syrupy poison that i return to
time and time again. i run from the day into the caress of the night
hide away from the sunshine. outside, empires may rise and fall,
tides may build and break, gardens may grow but
how would i know?
i'm here, in the dark
and i'm so, so tired.

6 days after Halloween: who are you

when you're on the edge of your bed
grief-gagged, sick to your
stomach and trying to find
a way to laugh about this?
or maybe you're too good at
that. maybe some things
weren't meant to be bright.
before you unwrap your can-
died pillowcase, ask yourself if
these pearl teeth you flash so
jack-o-lantern wide all the time
are bright like sun or bright like
scalpel?

Things I Know

I know life is war, and I think I'd let you
carve a trench in my belly if you thought it might
shield you from a bit of the fire–
if not the smoke than perhaps the flare;

I know life isn't fair, but I think I'd let you
write a lawbook down the pages of my spine,
dogear me and take me to court and crack me open
on the judge's podium to make it a bit more just;

I know life is just what it is, but I think I'd let you
tell me what I'm not until I rot, because even if it
hurts in the moment rot is really a soft little thing at its core,
and if it would help you grow just a few inches more...

I know life is a bore, but I think I'd let you
pour me into a red solo cup and splash me into the carpet,
fill me with ping pong balls and drunken laughter,
forget me on the kitchen counter,
and do it all over after the hangover tomorrow.

And I know maybe deep down somewhere in my marrow,
that doing all this only ends up in sorrow,
but it's easier, I think, to be soulless and used—
than be real and human and shoddy and bruised.
Because isn't it nicer to just be the sword
than one of the casualties
if life really is
war?

Of Shadows and Light

I loved you like sunlight,
but you only wanted
the darkness I couldn't give.
You built a home in the shadows,
and I stood at the threshold,
offering light you never asked for.
Perhaps some things aren't meant
to exist in the same sky.

hiraeth

these vowels tangle together awkwardly as though
something
was meant
to fit between them–

voice breaking in my throat,
i reach for some way to describe this maw inside of me
that used to be filled with something sweet that i can't
quite

remember?
those sweet days we chased cotton candy clouds with wide mouths,
imagining ourselves winged enough for the journey ahead and
counting the stars we never doubted we'd one day touch while
settling at the moment for the simple magics of life.
mouths sticky and bellies swollen, we did not even think to look back
until our bridges were already burned.

we didn't notice the matches striking
until the world caught fire behind us, and even then
we never thought to wonder about the heat at our backs until
the pain of pressing forward became
unbearable enough to search for a way out.

we were angels who'd
lost their wings along the way,
writhing as we learned that all along we'd been falling
calling it soaring until the moment we shattered on the earth below.

we thought ourselves untouchable
and now we can't bear to be touched
thrashing against constraint and comfort alike—

they say that an animal caught in a trap will gnaw off its own leg to get
free
forgetting
that humans are a species
bound, too, by animal instinct, and
what does that say about what we will do, when might becomes must?

in the end we will do what it takes to survive
even if what it takes is what will kill what's good in us
in the end.

hiraeth
longing
and oh how gruesomely we long

hiraeth
longing
and oh how futilely we try to reclaim

hiraeth
are we all simply homesick for heaven
missing our severed wings?

hiraeth
longing
and oh how humanly
we long.

ellipsis

No one tells you how sharp loneliness is. How it carves into you, leaves you raw and hollow, until even the sound of someone saying your name feels like a mercy. No one tells you that sometimes, it's not the ache that undoes you—it's the way the silence teaches you to hold it like a lover. The way the emptiness tucks itself under your tongue, kisses your palms, and waits.
                                      and   waits.
                                                                   and
                              waits.

                                                                         and

                                                                       waits…

Glass and Flame

You kissed me like fire,
but left like smoke.
Now I burn with questions
that no rain can drown.
Was I the wick,
or the spark?
And if I was the wick,
how could I have known
you only loved the fire
you could leave behind?

Said the phoenix

I've reached the point of no return,
the point of crash and burn;
they tell me live and learn,
but I am tired
of trying.

The climb to heaven hurts
and they tell me it's all about the journey anyway so
perhaps I'll give in to the freefall
to hell, eyes shut to the sins and ears open
to a music made for disintegration.

Let me lay among the night-dark leaves,
soak myself in whatever deliciously
heartbroken feeling exists down here.
I'll line my fingernails with potting soil,
hang the fruit and flowers by their stems so
only the scent remains.

Let my starlight bleed out until I
collapse into a black hole and
chew apart anyone who tries to
understand me.
Let them cower in the face of my
vastness, fall to their knees as my
gravity chokes out their light and
drags them to their demise.

Let me flip up my hood and drown
out the world, close the door on the best
parts of my life and close my eyes on
the pity and concern, and let me
think my bones hollow and dry
until I am nothing but kindling
waiting to be the start of some
devastation in this forest: something
irreversible.

And then. When there is nothing left.
When I am nothing but ashes and soot.

Let me open my eyes
and start again.

IV. Hope

Diamonds

they say diamonds are born of pressure,
        heat so relentless
        it bends carbon into
                brilliance.

                but no one speaks of the ash,
                  the dust left behind—
                soft, forgotten remnants
            that once shared the same origin.

i think about this as i hold a ring,
its diamond gleaming like a promise,
        sharp and cold,
perfect only because it   endured.

      and yet, i cannot help but wonder:
      is it the diamond that matters,
        or the dust it left
          behind?

        the world worships the hard, the unyielding,
          the things that shine under scrutiny.
            but what of the ash,
          the proof of transformation?
              it doesn't gleam,
            doesn't catch the light,
        but it knows the truth of ambition,
          the cost of   becoming.

perhaps we are both diamond and dust,
brilliance and the remnants of what we lost
to become it.

                            when we are gone,
                            what will remain?

the diamond may endure,
        a monument to resilience;

but the dust will dance,
carried by   the   breath   of   the   earth,
                                            soft and infinite,
                                    never bound to one form.

The Joy in Life is Death

there is a strange relief
in knowing it ends.
every step forward,
every breath pulled from the air,
is a march toward silence—
an unraveling of the weight
we were never meant to carry.

we hold life like a fragile thing,
terrified of the cracks
that creep along its edges.
but don't you see?
the cracks are what defines us.
they let the light escape.
they let the ending seep in
like water through stone.

death waits patiently,
a quiet shadow
that asks for nothing
but to be met.
and
in its waiting,
it gifts us urgency—
to love recklessly,
to hurt deeply,
to fill the hollow spaces
with something
before they empty again.

there is a joy in the knowing,
not because life is fleeting,
but because the fleeting is what makes it real.
because every goodbye,
every loss,
every breathless moment
we cannot hold onto
reminds us that this,
right now,
is all we have.

death is not an enemy.
it is a promise—

and maybe that's the joy.
not in life itself,
but in the quiet truth
that even the heaviest things
must one day
be put down.

as the seasons turn (ii)

after spring. after summer. after fall.

winter is left
to weather your pain.

she approaches quietly,
        eyes soft and sorrowful, snowshine smile pressed between blue
        lips pressed to your brokenness. she soothes you with frostbite
        forgiveness and a hand-stitched quilt of snow, silken and worn
        so thin that you think you can see yourself between stitches
        caught mid-laugh on a frosted windowpane,
        someone irrecoverable and

                                kind.

        you ache

        and when you build yourself up again with sticks and snow and
a carrot
        nose, you look at her with warm tears burning in your eyes
because you
        both know that what feels like healing now will only melt
        come springtime.

        winter simply catches your grief on her thumb and hands you
back
        diamonds. before you can bleed yet bluer, you look up to find
her fall-
        ing from every rooftop in the city, and you gasp at the plunging
shock of it,
        but after you finish crying out after her like a child, you will
find
        what she has left (you) behind:
        a blade of glass
        so you might fight back
                        next time.

presque vu

heartbeat of the world sucked so close to the surface
thrumming red and raw inches away
but your lashes cut it into slices and blur the edges
blink and it's gone.

there's a moment that lingers to drink down half a
cup of tea, nestling warmth into your chest,
and while it's there you take the time to bake something
sweet and crumbly. you're not a very good baker but
there's something about the right company that makes
your mess taste a bit marvelous.
you dab your mouth with the napkin;
blink and it's gone.

a mercurial pool of lucidity poured into the basin of your sink
staring down at red flowers blooming in the water and thinking
sad thoughts. you unplug the drain;
blink and it's gone.

staring contest with the moon
lazy-lidded eye, smug and sure
slitted-whites regarding you
with some semblance of interest
now that you're the only one looking back.
you try to keep yourself awake by dipping
your eyes into her craters, the scythe's line of her edge
but you'll always lose but once
and even then she's tight-lipped and smiling
as she refuses to give away her secrets
sinking behind a glittering ballgown sky
like a masquerade mask, fingertips reaching for the ribbons−!
blink and it's gone.

life

it arrives like frost—
quiet, breathless, settling into the bones of the world
before you even know to shiver.
a gasp carved from winter air,
the kind that scratches your throat raw
and leaves no proof of itself but the silence it breaks.

from that first inhale,
you belong to the waiting—
not for miracles, but for the subtle collapse
of who you were into who you almost became.

life is not galaxies or oceans.
it is smaller than that.
it is the steam that rises from your tea at 3:12 a.m.,
curling around your fingers like a ghost that forgot its name.
it is your reflection in a dark window—
distorted, soft-edged,
watching you watch yourself forget
how to want.

you chase meaning the way moths chase porchlight—
fumbling toward warmth that burns on contact.
you find it in hands that smell like smoke,
in doorframes that remember your shoulder,
in the pages of books that once knew you better than your own voice.

the ache becomes a rhythm,
a song you hum under your breath
because silence is heavier than melody.
longing turns feral,
something you cradle like a dying animal
because it's the only thing that still curls into you at night.

life won't answer.
it won't even turn to look.
it offers splinters—
moments sharp enough to open you.
you bleed, and call it memory.

and when it ends,
it will not shatter.
it will dissolve—
a final exhale into indifferent air.
no thunder, no thunder.

just the soft collapse of space
where you once folded the world around your body
and held it close,
as if that could make you stay.

The hush between storms where hope may take root.
Silence, a becoming.

the starry sky

the night is a cathedral,
vast and holy,
its ceiling studded with stars
that hum in a language older than god.
      i stand beneath it,
        small as a breath,
my silence swallowed by its immensity.

the stars do not blink.
          they burn,
their light a relic of a time
when the world was still learning   to   name   itself.

i wonder if they know
how they hold us together—
their cold fire stitching the sky
like seams on a fragile dress.

it is haunting, this beauty:
      how something so infinite
feels so intimately near,
     how the stars   linger
like ghosts of wishes i forgot to make.
their light pierces the dark,
sharp and silver,
yet soft enough to cradle the fragile hopes
i dare not speak
      aloud.

the wind carries the scent of forever,
     and i breathe it in,
          letting the vastness settle into my bones.

the stars don't promise answers,
don't tell stories with endings.

they only exist—
achingly distant,
achingly constant.

and yet,
beneath this quiet brilliance,
i   am   unmoored,
                as though the universe is whispering

                        that nothing was ever truly mine—

                        not the earth beneath my feet,
                 not the time slipping through my fingers,
                not even the love i clutch like a lifeline.

          the sky stretches, eternal,
                        and i feel its pull in my chest—
                a strange, aching gravity

that reminds me i, too, am stardust,

                a fragment of the infinite.
       and as the stars hum their ancient hymn,

                    i close my eyes,
                  letting their quiet song

                  unravel the edges of
                          who
                            i
                             am.

Advice from an Ember

I stood on the edge of the universe and saw myself staring back,
skin like the night sky, turn and stitched with silver scars,
eyes burning comets, daring me to break.

Do you dare touch the stars?
she asked, voice trembling, but not from fear—
from fury, from a longing too vast to hold in her ribs.

"I don't know if they'll burn."
The words spilled out, shameful, shaking, stupid.
She laughed, sharp and hollow.
Everything burns. You think you'll be the first not to?

Her fingers pointed to my chest, my throat, my soul.
You are the fire. You are the flare. You think you've been quiet all this time?
She grabbed me by the wrist, held it high against the void.
Look at you, carrying ash in your veins. Tell me—what are you saving it for?

I wanted to run, to turn back, to escape this unbearable confrontation—
but there was no running from her. No shadow to hide in. Not anymore.

Say it. Her voice cracked open, splintered into echoes.
Tell me you'd rather drown in your silence than ignite the night.
Tell me you'd rather be human than infinite.
Tell me you're scared, and I'dll still throw you in.

And for a moment, I hated her, hated her for seeing me,
for clawing the truth from my lungs like it was her birthright.
But beneath the hate was something smaller, rawer,
a spark I'd buried long ago.

"I'm tired," I whispered.
"Tired of touching things and watching them turn to smoke."
Her grip softened, her face crumbled into something familiar—
something mine.

Good, she said.
Let them burn. Let them crumble.
And then pick up what's left and make it yours.

She stepped back into the stars,
her silhouette a constellation,
a map carved into eternity.
& when I reached for her, for them, for the infinite,
the flames licked my hands,
and I laughed as I
burned.

On mirrors

The mirror doesn't lie, but it doesn't tell the truth, either.
It reflects only what it's given, and even then, it's incomplete.
The person staring back is always slightly wrong—
flattened, reversed, a version rendered in glass.
I watch her sometimes, unsure if she's watching back,
or just holding still because that's all she knows how.

There's a distance between surface and self,
between what is seen and what is meant.
The mirror offers edges, angles, outlines
but not the hush beneath a held breath,
not the pause before a word that never comes.

It can't catch the way silence sits in the body,
or how memory shifts its weight
depending on who's doing the looking.

And maybe that's its mercy.
Maybe we were never meant to be fully seen.

We are everything the mirror can't hold.

A cup of chai

steam curls like ghostly ribbons,
rising from the cup in my hands,
the scent of ginger and warmth
lingering in the air.

it is quite mundane, really;
leaves steeped in water, time distilled into something tangible.
the tea scalds my tongue, a small pain—sharp and fleeting—but
isn't it proof that i am alive? that i am able to
feel, to
burn, to
heal?

the leaves, too, have given themselves
to this ritual of becoming,
their essence unfurling
until nothing remains but what
haunts the bottom of the cup.
is that not what we all do?
spend ourselves in quiet ways,
pour our being into moments
that will fade into the next?

the world spins on outside this room,
loud and relentless,
but here,
the universe condenses;
into the swirl of tea and steam,
the delicate weight of the cup in my hands.
and for a moment,
i am enough.

My future

I can't wait to imagine my future
dream up every hope-drenched detail
paint it in pigments of the most calamitous colors
rub it blind and raw between widest eyes,
bleed flowerstains into it, make it something alive
and real, a glorious mirage over the lip of the horizon,
waiting across the endless, parched & gasping sands.

I can't wait to imagine it all,
every blisteringly beautiful bit of it,
and get it all wrong.

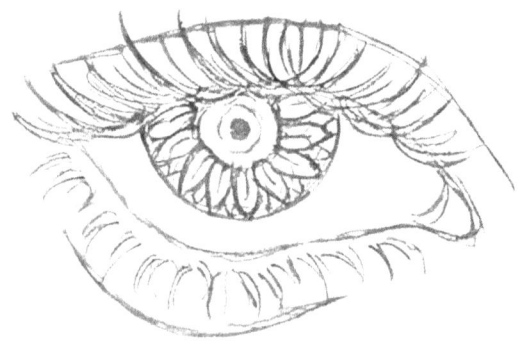

Poetry is My God

my jaw aches with words that don't exist. is this how you felt when you disgorged the world from your open mouth? there are pages and pages pressed to my lips and i'm trying not to swallow the ink, but my tongue and throat have been painted black. would a prayer wring me clean? you would say so, or maybe you wouldn't. i've heard of you one or twice, a million times, and they've told me so many things about you that the writing has gone over itself so many times it looks like nothing more than blotted ink. like ants crawling over the pages, swarming over their dead. their rotting bodies line the edges of my esophagus. their eyelash legs consume your face.

darling mine, i'd like to meet with you sometime untouched by the sun. i won't look if you open your mouth. i promise to listen. i promise to forget. i know some kiss your name into existence in smoke-stained air, and others close their eyes and trust that you'll dog their steps, blameless, nameless, and others still tie the stones of their grief to your ankles and call you an angel. but you and i both know better than to speak to those; the closest i've come to an angel is the impression my shoulderblades left in the mud where the snow melted away.

please. are you there? i need to talk to you. god i need to be understood and i think you're the only one to do it. and even if i don't hold god dear, i think it would be lovely for someone else to do it and know us in our entirety, but perhaps even more beautiful for them to know us in increments crumpled in sweaty palms, taken apart in order to be held recklessly by all. to imagine each of my shards on their own adventures is enough for me. is that how you feel? are you listening?

here, in the inexplicable, the unexplainable, the elusive uncapturable, here is where i am. meet me here, same time tomorrow? i have to tell you: i pity you. eternity must be a gruesome honor to endure. i'm sure i would not say this if i did know you; while the bonds of strangers are limitless, there are some truths we will never speak to our friends.

sincerely,

a girl you probably don't know either.

Epilogue

There's a story of a queen,
blessed by a witch to be
banished from the claws of mankind
and rule a land devoid of hatred.

They say she's been born a thousand times
and burned twice as many;
slipping to and from death
on borrowed breath.

She was jealously wreathed in
silk darker than sin,
legs spread, feet planted, most
certainly damned because how dare
she—*they hope she's sorry*—how dare she
regard the world with such a predator in her
eyes?

When she parted her blood-stained
lips and laughed, men were certain the
ugly noise could be naught but
a sign of evil; a crow's throaty cackle;
never considering what smoke
caused such a ruinous rasp.

And so the valiant villagers
rushed with swords raised
and prayers on their tongues,
certain steel could finish
what fire had failed to do;
certain of their purpose
although they knew not why
her death was required.

The men were returned with
slit throats and torn stomachs,
laid at the village gates,
warnings no one
dared to misread;
the women didn't return at all.

it was something of a cautionary tale
where the women are not slaughtered
but spared,
and the queen took them away
somewhere where they could break
themselves open in sanctity
and never be scorned:
somewhere where the fruit of their bodies
was borne for their lips alone.

(perhaps she will find peace someday,
this witch. or perhaps she already
has in a cycle of blood she has
mounted on her mantle,
a wound that will heal
in shades of vermillion).

Table of Contents

Prologue, Riley Killen & Vaani Tiwari — 1

I. Fury

    i am wrath, Vaani Tiwari — 5

    Anatomy of an Orchestra, Riley Killen — 6

    as her petals fell, Riley Killen — 7

    as i shattered, Vaani Tiwari — 9

    as the seasons turn (i), Riley Killen — 13

    the scream, Riley Killen — 14

    Supernova, Riley Killen — 15

    Iron & Fire, Vaani Tiwari — 17

    Quicksilver Girl, Riley Killen — 19

II. Darkness

    Flowers and Poison, Vaani Tiwari — 25

    unwanted, Riley Killen — 27

    gold and pyrite, Riley Killen & Vaani Tiwari — 29

    My mother's garden shears, Riley Killen — 30

    incandescent, Riley Killen — 31

applause, Vaani Tiwari	33
the hunger, Vaani Tiwari	35
The Hollow Ache of Absence, Vaani Tiwari	37
Skin Deep, Vaani Tiwari	39
Paper Cuts, Vaani Tiwari	40
Seams, Riley Killen	41
metamorphosis, Riley Killen	42

III. Burnout

kindness, Riley Killen	47
Sting, Vaani Tiwari	49
The Weight of Wings, Vaani Tiwari	50
Ash, Eventually, Vaani Tiwari	51
Yes., Riley Killen	53
Tired, Riley Killen	55
6 days after Halloween: who are you, Riley Killen	56
Things I Know, Riley Killen	57
Of Shadows and Light, Vaani Tiwari	58
hiraeth, Riley Killen	59
ellipsis, Vaani Tiwari	61

Glass and Flame, Riley Killen	62
Said the phoenix, Riley Killen	63

IV. Hope

Diamonds, Vaani Tiwari	69
The Joy in Life is Death, Vaani Tiwari	71
as the seasons turn (ii), Riley Killen	73
presque vu, Riley Killen	74
life, Vaani Tiwari	75
the starry sky, Vaani Tiwari	79
Advice from an Ember, Vaani Tiwari	81
On mirrors, Vaani Tiwari	83
A cup of chai, Vaani Tiwari	84
My future, Riley Killen	85
Poetry is My God, Riley Killen	86

Epilogue	91

Acknowledgements

So many people were involved in the process of this book becoming what it is today. We simply couldn't have made this a reality without all our lovely beta readers: Navya Chitlur, Audrey Shih, Reese Killen, Shree Vardhan, Jenna Jarrar, Aleeza Siddique, Ms. Doolittle, Miriam Frank, Keira Ching, and Ms. Masur. Thank you for taking the time to help make this book truer to itself.

A big thank you to Noor Latif, whose cover art gave our story it's first face. Your cover art is magnificent. To Boya, whose illustrations brought this world to life from the inside out; w. We admire your talent so much. Thank you both for working with us— we may be poets, but illustrations are definitely not our forte.

And finally, thank you tremendously to everyone who picked up this book and followed our journey to the end. To the readers; poetry would not be alive without you.

Riley:

I am deeply grateful to all the people who helped me become the person I needed to be to write this book— namely, Vaani Tiwari, my wonderful companion in writing who has read thousands of my words and told me to keep writing, Aurora Derrick, who never ceases to amaze me or make me laugh when I'm down, and Keira Ching, who reminds me life can be simple and full of love and silliness.

A special thanks to Ivy Qin and Ian Broihier, who believed in me, and Sophie Zeng, Bella Walter, Leah Edwards, Izzy Kellett, Victoria Deckard, and Alder Brandon for all of the shenanigans.

Thank you to everyone else who I have met along my writing journey: Erika Luckert, Kate Delay, Que Avery, Charlie Dai, Briana Escobar, Bach Le, Madeline Obadiah, Lucy Ren, Saskia Sommer, Ananya Upadhye, Richard Zhang, Benjamin Lancor, Charisma Holly, Izzie Elfont-Caradonna, Alejandra Guzman, and Annika Dowdall— you have inspired me, uplifted me, and taught me so much more than you know.

Thank you especially to Reese, my ultimate partner in crime. And finally, thank you forever to Mom and Dad, who don't quite understand poetry but love and support me without fail. I wouldn't have made it here without you, and I love you both to the moon and back.

All my love,
        Riley

Vaani:

I owe more than I can neatly name to the people who made this book possible, and will have to settle, instead, for naming a few. To Riley Killen, my brilliant co-author and one of the rare people whose sentences I trust as much as her judgment; to Aurora Derrick, who has seen every part of me and stayed, the truest friend a girl could hope for; and to Satvika Satish, whose talent, humor, and dedication have made our friendship both effortless and enduring— thank you.

To the alumni and faculty of CSSSA 2024, especially my roomates: thank you for revealing that the world is, despite everything, full of poetry. To my wonderful friends (Emilia Smith, Noor Latif, Jenna Jarrar, Uma Harihan, Gabby Hildebrand, Milena Foreman, Nour Ghanem, Aleeza Siddique, Fatemah Ali, Shree Vardhan, Jewel Sudnagunta, Reese Shelton, Laurel Xu, & all those I haven't named), thank you for always supporting me.

My deepest thanks go to the adults who named me a writer before I fully believed it myself: Mr. O'Cyrus, Ms. Anna Casalme, and Ms. Jonelle Patrick. Thank you to Ms. Hale for showing me no matter how busy life gets, there's always time to read.

And finally, thank you to my family. My brother, steadfast through every chaos; my puppy Lila, for permitting my affections even when she clearly had better things to do; and my parents, for their endless love, which has always been the beginning and the end of everything.

xxx Vaani

Riley Killen is a junior at Truckee High. Her work has been featured in Stone Soup literary magazine and the 2025 Kenyon Young Writers Anthology. Riley loves reading and walking her dog (sometimes simultaneously) and can often be found making strange smoothies. In her free time, she adds to her chaotically curated Spotify playlist, puts it on shuffle, and sings along.

Vaani Tiwari is a high school student who spends most of her time chasing sentences and occasionally catching them. She is the author of poetry collections *Perfect on Paper* and *Call Me A Witch,* as well as historical novella *The War From Dusk Till Dawn.* Her work can also be found in the *Youth Takeover Magazine*, *CSSSA Literary Magazine*, and *The Persimmon Review*. A Governor's Medallion of the Arts recipient and California State Summer School for the Arts alum, she is invited to speak at the 2026 San Francisco Writers Conference.

Vaani loves fantasy, sending essay-length messages to her long-distance friends, and conversations about how everything is fleeting and therefore, inconveniently, beautiful. One day she plans to practice medicine; in the meantime, she is busy diagnosing characters with feelings.

Boya Liu is an artist who discovered her love for art at a young age and draws for enjoyment. Beginning from scribbles of unicorns on multicolored paper, she has developed her artistic skills through consistent practice with different mediums and art styles. To her, art is an escape from the world and a form of relaxation. Although she has not taken formal art classes, she often enjoys drawing from references found on the internet and in her surroundings. She believes symbolic drawings are also important to visually expressing and clarifying complex emotions, as demonstrated by the illustrations in the book. Outside of her artistic hobbies, she enjoys playing tennis and trying new foods. Boya hopes to continue drawing as a hobby in the future in addition to her other plans.

www.ingramcontent.com/pod-product-compliance
Lightning Source LLC
Chambersburg PA
CBHW051346040426
42453CB00007B/439